THE SUM OF ME

A Memoir

Mark Brundage Odom

Copyright ©2024 by Mark Brundage Odom.

All rights reserved. No part of this book may be reproduced, stored in a retrieval system, or transmitted in any form or by any means without the prior written permission of the publisher—except by a reviewer who may quote brief passages in a review to be printed in a newspaper, magazine, or journal.

For privacy reasons, some names, locations, and dates may have been changed.

Published by
A&M Publishing

Book Cover and Interior Design by
www.TWA Solutions.com

ISBN: 979-8-9888648-0-6 (Paperback)
ISBN: 979-8-9888648-1-3 (eBook)

For inquiries, contact the publisher.

Manufactured in the United States of America

Distributed by
Ingram Content
www.ingramcontentgroup.com

Visit Mark Brundage Odom online
www.markbrundageodom.com

To my wife, Ariane Odom, whose unwavering support and enduring love are my pillars of strength. She is my eternal source of encouragement and inspiration.

Acknowledgments

Ross Swann, author of *Six Years of Reckless Poppin*, for being a positive influence in telling me to keep going and never give up.

Toni Brundage, my newly found sister, for supporting me and answering so many questions that filled in the many gaps of information.

Aaron Hough, my newly found brother, inspired me, through his journey, to want to know more about where I came from.

Marilyn Loving inspired me to use Ancestry search to locate my relatives and explore a wealth of information.

Roderick Odom, my steadfast partner on this journey called life, has always regarded me as nothing less than his big brother.

Contents

Introduction 1

Chapter One: My Beginning... 7

Chapter Two: My Childhood, or Lack Of.. 13

Chapter Three: My Pittsburgh Connection 17

Chapter Four: The Man I Called "Dad" 32

Chapter Five: Transitions and Turbulence 35

Chapter Six: "You're Just the Bastard" 40

Chapter Seven: California Dreamin'................................. 54

Chapter Eight: Back on the Porch 61

Chapter Nine: Louisiana Bound 64

Chapter Ten: Gaining My Independence........................ 73

Chapter Eleven: Enter Roy Waiters 76

Chapter Twelve: Feeling Unloved..................................... 79

Chapter Thirteen: Tracing Roots and Family Secrets 83

Chapter Fourteen: Navigating Secrets and the

    Quest for Truth 101

Chapter Fifteen: Walking in Faith 105

Chapter Sixteen: My Two Sons 111

Chapter Seventeen: My Ride or Die…and
    Then Some.. 116

Chapter Eighteen: Mom and the
    Next Generations 123

Conclusion: Hidden Truths... 129

Family.. 135

About the Author.. 149

"My circumstances whence I came do not define me."

~Mark Brundage Odom

INTRODUCTION

I grew up with a quiet yet persistent ache in my heart. From my earliest recollections, the mystery of paternal absence shrouded my life, casting a long shadow over my formative years.

Mark Joseph Odom, a name that bore the weight of a story untold, a history fragmented, was a testament to the complexities of family and the profound influence of those who were missing. In a world where lineage and ancestry intertwined like the roots of an ancient oak tree, my existence was akin to a book missing chapters, a symphony with an unfinished melody.

In my adolescence, I learned that the only dad I knew was not my biological father. I knew nothing about my biological father. As I ventured further into adolescence, the questions burgeoned within me like a garden of unanswered riddles. Who was this elusive man? Why had he vanished from my life, leaving only a void where paternal guidance should have flourished?

My mother raised me, carrying the weight of single parenthood for the first two years of my life, until she married Joshua Odom, who I believed was my biological father until I discovered the truth.

Yet, the absence of paternal presence was a relentless companion, a nagging uncertainty that followed me through the seasons of my life. There were questions my mother would not answer, stories she would not tell.

At fifty-seven, I stood on the precipice of a life-altering journey, one that would take me deep into the labyrinthine corridors of my identity. This journey would define me, challenge me, and ultimately lead me to a profound revelation that transcended the boundaries of family and blood.

The Sum of Me is my memoir that navigates the intricate tapestry of my life, drawing attention to the profound impact of growing up without knowing my biological father and, by extension, siblings and paternal grandparents, whose existence remained a mystery. It is a story that unfolds within the intricate dance of identity and heritage, where the absence of one branch of my family tree casts a long shadow over my self-discovery.

In a quest to unearth the missing pieces of my lineage, I grapple with the emotions, complexities, and revelations that come with confronting the shadows of the past. *The Sum of Me* is a testament to the resilience of the human spirit and the enduring search for a sense of belonging, identity, and completeness in the face of a missing paternal legacy.

The decision to embark on a journey to find my missing paternal lineage didn't come in a single, thunderous epiphany. Instead, it was a gradual realization that had been quietly taking root within me for years, nurtured by the seeds of curiosity and the gnawing void left by my absent biological father.

As I entered my pre-teenage years, my curiosity about my father intensified. It was the little things that triggered it—friends talking about their dads, seeing fathers and sons share knowing smiles, or when told I was a bastard.

The flood of questions that surged within me was overwhelming. Where was he? Why didn't he look for me? What kind of person was he?

However, it wasn't just about satisfying my curiosity. There was a deeper emotional drive at play. As I navigated the treacherous waters of adolescence, the absence of a male role model became glaringly evident. I yearned for guidance, for someone to teach me the unspoken lessons of manhood, and to fill the void left by his absence. I had my dad, but he was emotionally absent and could answer none of my questions. I also did not ask many questions for fear of how it would make him feel.

There was an element of validation in my quest. I had often wondered if my biological father's absence reflected my inadequacy or unworthiness. Finding him, and understanding why he had left when I was born, would be a way to quell those insecurities and affirm my sense of self-worth.

The Sum of Me

In the chapters that followed, I would recount the obstacles and challenges I encountered in my search for answers, the emotional rollercoaster that came with each lead and setback, and the impact this quest had on my identity and self-esteem.

CHAPTER ONE

My Beginning

In 1965, Pittsburgh, Pennsylvania, was a thriving industrial city, known for its steel mills and other manufacturing industries. The population of the city was around six-hundred-thousand people, with many more living in the surrounding metropolitan area.

One of the major events of 1965 in Pittsburgh was the completion of the Gateway Center, a complex of modernist office buildings and hotels in downtown Pittsburgh. This development was a symbol of the city's progress and economic growth.

However, Pittsburgh was also facing significant social and economic challenges during this time. The decline of the steel industry, which had been a cornerstone of the city's economy for many years, was taking its toll. Unemployment was on the rise, and many residents were struggling to make ends meet.

The civil rights movement was also making its presence felt in Pittsburgh, with local activists working to end discrimination and segregation in housing, employment, and education. In August 1965, a group of African American protesters staged a sit-in at a downtown department store, demanding an end to racial discrimination in hiring practices.

Despite these challenges, Pittsburgh remained a vibrant city in 1965, with a rich cultural scene that included world-class museums, theaters, and music venues. The Pittsburgh Pirates baseball team was also enjoying a successful season, winning the National League pennant and competing in the World Series. Also, the Pittsburgh Steelers, in 1965, finished with a record of two wins, twelve losses, and no titles, which placed them last in the Eastern Conference. The 1965 season was the Steelers' thirty-third season in the NFL, and their fourth under head coach, Mike Nixon. *Go, Steelers!*

Also in Pittsburgh, on July 31, 1965, I was born to Rachel Ann Walden and to a man whom I would learn about some fifty years later. Other than the pieces I have put together over the years, I still haven't solved the puzzle surrounding my birth, and I never will. However, I'm okay with that because with what I've learned so far, I now know who I am and whose I am.

A Broken Branch…

I am not heavy on genealogy. I prefer asking family members questions, hoping to receive truthful answers. However, I also recognize that, like me, not everyone knows the truth. During the time I was born, and throughout my childhood, my family held secrets close to the chest. Many took those secrets to the grave. In genealogy, a "broken branch" on a family tree refers to where one cannot trace his lineage or if it is unknown. This can occur for a variety of reasons, including incomplete or missing records, adoption, estrangement, or disownment. It is also important to note that a broken branch does not mean that the person or their descendants are not part of the family; it simply means there is a gap in the family tree where information is missing. This is my case.

From the moment I was born until 2019, I had several broken—more like missing—branches on my family tree. I was not completely in the dark. Even though I knew my maternal side of the family, my paternal was a mystery. I did not know my biological father's name or if I had other siblings. I knew nothing. However, I had a wonderful stepfather, whom you will meet in a later chapter. The following are branches to my tree that I know are intact, with a few surprises.

My maternal great-grandparents were Benjamin and Gladys Ernestine Hudson Bracey. Gladys lived to the age of one hundred-two. With the loss of her eyesight, she had phenomenal insight and wisdom when it came to people. Benjamin was a railroad worker who died on January 8, 1954, at fifty-two years old from a coronary heart attack.

My maternal grandmother, Indiana Pantheris Bracey, was born October 9, 1922, in Dinwiddie, Virginia. In 1942, Indiana gave birth to my mother, Rachel Ann—last name unknown. My biological grandfather remains a mystery. It is probably a mystery for my mother, too.

On November 24, 1943, Indiana married Johnnie Roland "Buddy" Walden in Cochise, Arizona. Later, my grandparents would welcome my uncles: Johnnie Jr., and Charles. Grandmother Indiana died on December 18, 1954, eleven months after her father, Benjamin Bracey. She died from myocarditis, leaving her husband to raise their children.

Losing a parent at any age is traumatic and can be a life-altering experience. It can also have a profound impact on a young girl who loses her mother at twelve years old. Although Mom and I have never discussed it, I am sure my grandmother's passing took an emotional and maybe a psychological toll on her. If Mom's relationship with her mother was anything like her relationship with my sister, Nikki, I am sure they were best of friends and confidantes and did everything together. Fortunately, Hopewell, Virginia, remained home for her. Her aunts, uncles, and family loved her as if she were their own. They may have overcompensated and spoiled her.

After Grandmother Indiana died, I do not know how long after my grandfather, Johnnie Walden Sr., married his second wife, Dorothy L. Marshall. Mom lived with her father and stepmother in Pittsburgh. From this union were Annette and a set of twins, Yvonne and Yvette, my mother's half-sisters.

Living in Pittsburgh with her father and stepmother, Mom did her schooling and worked in a hospital. She also met my biological father. In 1964, Mom learned she was pregnant with me. Through an Ancestry search, I found the marriage license from Virginia between Rachel Ann Walden and Joseph Brundage on June 4, 1965, almost two months before my birth on July 31, 1965. Why they chose Winchester, Virginia, to marry remains a mystery. My biological father's name was Joseph Brundage. My middle name is Joseph. That may not seem paramount to some, but for me, it was huge. It is quite the important missing piece of the puzzle that is me.

CHAPTER TWO

My Childhood, or Lack of...

As far as childhood, I never had one. I was born to a parent who was always busy with work and other commitments, and she had little time to spend with me. As a result, and with a few exceptions, I grew up feeling neglected by my mother. Unintentional, of course; at least that is what I would like to believe. Grandmother Indiana died when Mom was at a young age—around twelve. Losing a mother as a child can be an incredibly painful experience. Losing their mothers as children can leave a lasting impact on their lives, as children depend on them for love, support, and guidance. They may also have difficulty processing their emotions and may feel like they have to grow up too quickly to compensate for the loss. I believe this may be why my mother could not provide me with the love and support I needed—because she didn't know how to give it.

Living in Pittsburgh, Mom never thought of it as home. Soon after I was born, she learned that my biological father, whom she had married in Winchester, Virginia, was already married with a family living in Pittsburgh. He had two children: Joseph, Jr., and Toni. Yes, he already had a son named Joseph. I'm sure it was devastating for Mom. She called Uncle Junnie, who drove from Hopewell, Virginia, to Pittsburgh, to pick us up and bring us to Hopewell. We took up refuge with her maternal family. I would later learn my biological father wanted to take me and raise me, which was another reason for our departure.

In Hopewell, we lived with my mother's maternal grandmother, Gladys Bracey, and my great aunt Carrie, Gladys' only living daughter. Hopewell holds some very great memories for me. I never had what you might call a normal childhood, growing up with two parents, grandparents, and other relatives who had my back; I had no real support system. I won't have a family that shares secrets, so I do not have secrets to pass down to my children. Every family has secrets. Some scar you for life and others leave you ashamed and broken. Then there are those you just know about.

Mom got a job in a hospital. Then, she met and married Joshua Odom in February 1967. He was in the Army and he was the only father I had ever known. After they married, he adopted me, giving me his last name: Odom. I proudly wrote my name "Odom" all those years, never knowing it wasn't really mine. It was years before I would know this information firsthand. Then, my parents gave me the best gift ever: a brother. Roderick was born in October 1967.

My fondest memories of a true family started around age four. We were on a train, bound for Germany. Dad had joined the Army at a relatively young age to get away from his past. He was the oldest of nine children born to Samuel Douglas Odom and Vastie Thomas Odom. Supposedly, Samuel was not Joshua's biological father. Remember, I said some secrets scare you!

I love having a younger brother. He has been my best friend and confidant since we could talk. We tell each other anything. I remember once we drank our father's beer when he got up to use the bathroom. Each time he would go to the bathroom, our mother caught us taste-testing our father's beer. Most parents would have confronted their children, but not my parents. My father sat us down and made us drink a beer each. What a horrible decision that was for me.

CHAPTER THREE

My Pittsburgh Connection

Johnnie Roland Walden, Sr., affectionately known as Buddy, was a remarkable man and my maternal grandfather. He was born on April 16, 1920, in Skippers, Virginia, to the late Willie Walden and Stevie Carpenter Walden. His indelible mark extended from Skippers, Virginia, to the city of Pittsburgh, Pennsylvania. With unwavering determination and an entrepreneurial spirit, Buddy pursued tailoring as a trade and established his own tailor shop. He became a prominent figure, symbolizing success for African Americans, breaking barriers, and paving the way for future generations of entrepreneurs. He also attained the esteemed rank of a 33rd Degree Mason, reflecting his commitment to the Masonic Order.

Buddy's courage led him to enlist in the United States Army during World War II, where he served in the esteemed African-American Cavalry Regiment known as the Buffalo Soldiers. As a staff sergeant, he committed himself wholeheartedly to his military duties. His exceptional service earned him several distinguished military decorations, including the Good Conduct Ribbon, American Theater Service Ribbon, and World War II Victory Ribbon. In recognition of his invaluable service to his country, he received an honorable discharge.

My maternal grandfather was a Buffalo Soldier, an intriguing fact. The Buffalo Soldiers were a group of African-American soldiers who served in the United States Army after the Civil War. The origin of their name has differing theories—one suggesting that their dark, curly hair resembled buffalo fur, and another associating their bravery and ferocity with buffalo. Regardless, this name was high praise, as the Native people of the Great Plains deeply respected buffalos. In

1866, an Act of Congress established six all-Black peacetime regiments, later merged into four: the 9th and 10th Cavalry and the 24th and 25th Infantry.

Buddy exchanged vows with Indiana Pantheris Bracey on November 24, 1943, in Cochise, Arizona. Indiana, born on October 9, 1922, in Dinwiddie, Virginia, remains a mystery regarding her upbringing, education, and early life. My sense of yearning and intrigue toward her is only natural, given her significant role in my family's history. She gave birth to my mother, Rachel Ann, and uncles, Johnnie Jr. and Charles.

Sadly, Indiana passed away at thirty-two. Her untimely death left her husband to raise three young children.

In my family's complex history, there are certain aspects I've wanted to explore further. One of these is the story of my grandmother, Indiana Bracey. Despite her passing before I got to meet her, I often think about the lessons she could have taught, the stories she might have shared, and how she could have influenced my development. Her absence leaves me reflecting on what it would have been like to know her and the potential impact of her wisdom on my life.

As I grew older, I discovered that Buddy Walden was not my biological maternal grandfather. The identity of my actual maternal grandfather remains a mystery, and it is unlikely that I will ever uncover it. In my heart and mind, Buddy Walden will forever be my grandfather. His influence and presence have significantly shaped who I am today.

Later, Buddy married Dorothy L. Marshall. From that union, Annette and twins Yvonne and Yvette were born. I did not perceive Dorothy as a step-grandmother during my childhood, as I was oblivious to the concept of step-relationships. What mattered was that she was married to the man I knew as my grandfather, and she deeply cared for me, and our bond made her my grandmother.

Dorothy embodied kindness, compassion, and love in every interaction. Beyond nurturing, she emphasized the importance of faith in God and self-belief. She encouraged us to discover and pursue our passions while valuing education. Self-definition held great significance for both Dorothy and Buddy, and education was a shared priority among my grandparents.

Dorothy's faith shone brightly, and she had a deep love

for the church, remaining engaged in its activities. She taught Sunday School and was a vital part of the church choir, mesmerizing everyone with her angelic voice.

Dorothy was a living gospel legend. She was a beacon of musical inspiration in the Greater Pittsburgh metropolitan area for over sixty years, earning national recognition for her soul-stirring gospel singing. Her musical journey began at nine years old, with her first solo being the heartfelt rendition of "I Love to Tell the Story of Jesus."

As a young adult, Dorothy became a vital part of the Humble Five, a musical group established by the Howard family of Macedonia Baptist Church. She lent her voice to the Mount Zion Singers, the Mary Johnson Davis Singers, and the Pittsburgh Chorale Union, an esteemed institution affiliated with the National Convention of Choirs and Choruses founded by the late Thomas A. Dorsey.

Dorothy's commitment to musical excellence extended beyond her performances. She was a member of the Hampton University Ministers' Conference and the Choir Directors and Organists Guild, having also served on its executive board. As a past-worthy matron of Bethsheba, Chapter #25 Order of Eastern Stars, Dorothy displayed unwavering dedication to her community.

Throughout her musical journey, Dorothy received many tributes and honors, including recognition for twenty-five years of service in the Pittsburgh Chorale Union, a certificate from the James Cleveland Workshop as one of Pittsburgh's legendary Gospel singers, and a plaque commemorating her thirty-two years of service in the Hampton's Choir Guild.

Her active involvement in the music department under various pastoral leadership reflected her devotion to Macedonia Baptist Church, spanning over six decades. Dorothy served as the director of the Macedonia Baptist Church Gospel Choir for an impressive thirty-five years and played a pivotal role in organizing the Male Chorus.

Under the leadership of Reverend Pugh, she served as director of Kingdom Kids at Macedonia and continued to contribute her talents to the Shekina Choir and the Shalom Ensemble, delivering soul-stirring solos when called upon.

Beyond her musical accomplishments, Dorothy was a devoted wife to my grandfather, Johnnie R. Walden, a mother to six children, a grandmother, and a great-grandmother. Her favorite colors, purple and lavender, reflected her vibrant spirit. The rose was her preferred flower, and the hymn "Great Is Thy Faithfulness" held a special place in her heart. Her favorite gospel selection, "I Won't Complain," resonated deeply.

Above all else, Dorothy wanted the world to know that she was a child of God, and that throughout the years, God had been abundantly good to her. Her life's anthem echoed with gratitude: "If it had not been for the Lord on her side, where would she be?"

Dorothy had a talent for crafting the most delicious lemonade. As a devoted homemaker, she showered her family with love, care, and a sense of warmth and happiness.

A captivating oil painting nestled above the fireplace mantle in Buddy and Dorothy's home depicted the legendary Buffalo Soldiers in a resplendent gold frame. This artwork held immense beauty and also ignited curiosity among guests who entered the room. It provided an opportunity for Buddy to share his personal narrative intertwined with the remarkable legacy of the Buffalo Soldiers.

As guests admired the painting's intricate details, the bravery and resilience of these historic African American soldiers came to life. Buddy seized this opportunity to recount their heroic tales, honoring their legacy. His passionate storytelling, coupled with his command of Italian phrases, lent authenticity and depth to the narrative, transporting listeners to an era of courage and sacrifice. The Buffalo Soldiers depicted in the painting symbolized more than art—they embodied a significant chapter in Buddy's life.

Buddy's passion for the Italian language extended beyond his home. While fulfilling his duties at the bank, he engaged customers of Italian origin in conversations, maintaining his language proficiency and cultivating meaningful relationships.

Dorothy was a powerhouse with an anointed voice. She traveled the nation as part of a gospel group and met Granddaddy during one of her tours at a Virginia church. Their connection led to a long-distance relationship, culminating in his decision to marry her and move from his hometown to Pittsburgh.

Dorothy's power often manifested through her silence. What remained concealed for many years was her ability to influence through reticence. She held crucial information but refrained from revealing it directly. Instead, both she and

Granddaddy left subtle breadcrumbs, believing my mother, Rachel, bore the responsibility of caring for me. Their restraint emerged even as my mother allowed me to cry and struggled with postpartum depression, making ill-fated choices.

They exercised restraint, with Granddaddy at times pulling Grandma back from intervening in my care. Their shared secrets and lies strained their relationship with my mother, making them complicit in silence. Granddaddy, an inspirational figure to many men and a dedicated Mason, bore this silent burden into his eighties. Imagine the internal struggle he faced, unable to fully contribute to my growth and understanding of my origins—knowledge that held immense value to both Granddaddy and Grandma, who served as torchbearers for every family reunion.

They meticulously preserved family documents and history, dedicating substantial effort to compiling books and booklets for family reunions. Their intent was to pass on this legacy to me, but the weight of my mother's silence restricted their aspirations. This silence played a significant role in shaping their actions, showcasing how deeply they valued these truths. As I evolved into an adult with a family of my own, I witnessed how their dreams of imparting this knowledge were thwarted, leaving their interactions incomplete.

At one point, Granddaddy even disclosed that he knew where my family lived. He extended an offer to accompany me to meet them, but I wasn't ready to embrace that journey, even at forty-five years old because of fear of rejection and bad timing due to employment obligations.

I visited Pittsburgh when I attended the G-20 Summit hosted there. I was on duty and squeezed in some free time during my day shift. During that visit, I went to my grandfather's house, revisiting the place that held so much history and significance.

During my childhood summers in Pittsburgh, I cherish countless memories of times spent with family. However, one particular incident has etched itself into my mind forever. In the 1970s, unlike today, fire alarms were conspicuous fixtures mounted on street poles, easily seen and accessible to all. Encased in sturdy enclosures, typically made of metal or a metal-glass combination, these alarms withstood the elements. A simple pull of the handle or lever was all it took to set off a distinct sound, promptly alerting the neighborhood of a fire or emergency, serving as crucial safety measures.

Regrettably, these alarms also enticed mischievous children like us who were in search of excitement during those carefree summer days. One fateful day, my cousins, Johnnie, Jr., and Steven, along with my brother Rick and me, succumbed to a temptation that was too strong to resist. With a mixture of curiosity and mischief in our hearts, we unwittingly wreaked havoc. Little did we know the consequences that would follow.

That incident marked a significant turning point, for it was the first time Dorothy felt compelled to discipline me. The memory of her stern reprimand and the swiftness of her disciplinary actions still lingers in my mind. Although it was a lesson learned the hard way, it serves as a reminder of the importance of responsibility, understanding the consequences of our actions, and respecting the safety measures put in place for the well-being of the community.

Through this unforgettable experience, I not only gained a profound respect for the significance of fire alarms and their role in safeguarding lives, but also learned a valuable lesson about the consequences of yielding to impulsive temptations—thanks to Dorothy.

Our family reunion bears the mark of Granddaddy's careful organization. He played a pivotal role in shaping its structure, with different family members hosting it in alternating years across various states. I remember one year when it took place in Baltimore, Maryland. It was during this event that we received the family history book.

Granddaddy had a fervor for delving into our family's lineage. This passion extended to researching our history. While poring through historical records, an astonishing revelation emerged. My wife's nickname, Arie, takes on various forms such as Ariane. Her version, Arie, carries special significance. However, as we delved into our family's past, we uncovered an astounding connection: four generations ago, my grandmother had the same name as my wife, Arie, spelled exactly the same. The other common denominator with us is that she was a Native American, like my wife. I was taken aback by this remarkable coincidence.

Granddaddy's commitment to meticulous research and orderliness extended even to his basement, which he transformed into an office. This space mirrored the diligence he applied to every aspect of his life, under the guidance of his faith and God's direction. His unwavering dedication was clear not only in his work for the Masonic organization and the church, but also in his tireless efforts for the family.

One day, my wife, Ariane, and I were driving down Interstate 95, going to a family reunion. We were making good time at around ninety-five miles per hour. We were determined to arrive swiftly, albeit in a controlled manner. As we cruised along the highway, a burgundy Cadillac in the right lane caught my attention as it zoomed past us. What stood out was the license plate that bore the word "BLESSED," a signature touch that was unmistakably Grandma's.

Granddaddy owned a burgundy Suburban. It was a true gem, meticulously cared for, and he always kept it in impeccable condition. Despite his age, which was well into his late eighties and early nineties, he was still driving it. He died at ninety-five years old.

Upon Granddaddy's passing, the truck found a new home with Uncle Junie, who ensured its pristine condition. This cherished vehicle has now entered the hands of the third generation, Granddaddy's grandson. The transition occurred when he moved from a house with a two-car garage to a condo, driven by his passion for cars, yet still maintaining a garage for his new Audi. Thus, the truck continued its journey through the family.

I can't overlook my connection with Uncle Junie, my mom's brother. From my earliest memories until now, he's been a reliable support, holding me down in various ways. Growing up, alongside my adoptive dad, Joshua Odom, Uncle Junie played a crucial fatherly role in my life.

His influence goes beyond the usual family stuff, forming a connection based on respect and shared experiences. He's been a guide, shaping my understanding of manhood and responsibilities. Beyond the family label, Uncle Junie became a mentor, passing on practical life lessons.

Aside from the care he gave me, Uncle Junie showed the importance of resilience, hard work, and compassion. His actions spoke volumes, teaching the qualities of a man of character. His example taught me about integrity, perseverance, and the strength that comes from genuine connections.

Uncle Junie wasn't just an uncle to me; he was like a father, a mentor, someone I could always rely on, and a trusted confidant. Looking back, I realize how instrumental

The Sum of Me

Uncle Junie was in molding me into the person I am today. He remains my go-to person for advice and guidance, always offering a voice of reason. Our love for motorcycles and cars still bonds us.

CHAPTER FOUR

The Man I Called "Dad"

Throughout my life, the man I knew as my dad was Joshua Odom, the person who was my father through adoption. He became the core father figure in my world, the one I affectionately called "Dad." Dad stepped in to fill a role that might have otherwise felt empty, showing that a biological connection wasn't necessary to create a strong and meaningful bond. He was all I knew for thirteen years, and I was happy with that. A day doesn't go by that I don't think of him.

As I grew up, the mystery surrounding my biological father's identity lingered, wrapped in uncertainty and unanswered questions. Over time, I came to terms with the idea that I might never get to know or understand who my birth father was. The desire to uncover his story, to find out where I came from, and to potentially meet him, became a puzzle piece that seemed forever missing from my life's journey.

The absence of this knowledge left a lasting impact, a kind of ache that emerged during moments of reflection. But amid this longing, I came to the realization that genetics do not solely define the concept of fatherhood. Joshua Odom proved that being my dad goes beyond biology—it's about shared experiences, shared values, and the emotional connection that develops. His unwavering presence shaped my sense of family and belonging.

With time, I also grasped the idea that fatherhood is more than just blood relations. It's about the care, guidance, and emotional connection that a person provides. Even though the identity of my biological father might always remain a mystery, it's Joshua Odom's impact that truly shaped my life. He showed me that a father's love and support are not bound by biology, but grounded in the depth of a meaningful relationship.

In life's broader context, the unknown details about my biological father don't diminish the concrete care and dedication provided by Joshua Odom. His influence shaped how I see fatherhood and family, guiding me through life's complexities with a love that surpasses biology.

CHAPTER FIVE

Transitions and Turbulence

Following our time in Germany, our family moved to Dugway, Utah, between 1970 and 1971, as it was the next destination for Dad's military deployment. It was in Dugway that I not only started my early education but also enthusiastically became a part of several sports teams, including swimming, baseball, and basketball. This transition marked a pivotal period in my life, as I not only adjusted to a new environment but also began developing my academic and athletic interests.

After residing in Germany since the age of two and immersing myself in the local culture, I formed a deep connection to the German way of life. To where I genuinely believed I had German roots before I set foot back in the United States. However, a significant turning point came in Utah, as it was there that I had an eye-opening revelation: I am, in fact, of African-American heritage.

Rick and I enrolled in a school in Utah, where we had plenty of bonding time with our dad. It was also during this time that an incident occurred involving Dad.

He had a history of binge drinking, but this event escalated to a physical altercation with Mom, where he put his hands on her. It wasn't in his nature to be violent, but I'm talking about a drunken brawl, and it was the first time I had ever seen him put his hands on someone, especially Mom. The domestic violence incident involved pushing and Dad putting his hands on her throat, not a physical hit. Still, that infuriated me, totally pissed me off. So, I confronted him and told him, "You shouldn't do that, it's not cool. Especially to my mother."

That was her breaking point, so Mom and Dad went their separate ways. Even though he didn't want to leave the marriage. He loved Mom very much. However, for Mom, that marked the end of their relationship, so Dad moved out.

My father, a veteran of the Vietnam War, carried the heavy burden of traumatic experiences from that conflict, a burden shared by many who served during that era. The scars of war, compounded by the challenges of alcoholism and various other hardships, cast a pervasive shadow over the lives of many veterans during those times. The aftermath of the Vietnam War left a lasting impact on those who served, and it was not uncommon for them to grapple with a complex web of physical, emotional, and social difficulties. These challenges often went unaddressed or misunderstood, underscoring the profound and enduring toll that war could take on the lives of those who have served.

Eventually, Dad left Utah, marking the start of a big change for our family. Mom packed up our stuff as we got ready for a long road trip back to Virginia. We squeezed into our small Volkswagen Beetle, determined to cover the many miles. This happened during a tough time when my parents had separated, and I was just starting third grade. After we reached Virginia, the car was repossessed almost immediately, but this was after we slept in the car because Mom felt embarrassed about revealing the reason for our sudden return.

While in Virginia, Allen entered the picture. Allen was in the military, too. He was a nice guy, stationed at Ft. Eustis in Newport News, Virginia, and I liked him. He drove a blue Buick Electra 225 with a white top and blue crushed velvet seats. He taught me how to drive, about the gear shifts: reverse, neutral, drive, first, and second.

Mom and Allen dated, and during this time, Dad's sister, Aunt Mary, also lived with us in Virginia. So, she saw Mom with Allen, witnessed their interactions, and contacted her brother to inform him of what was going on. This brought Dad to Virginia. He wanted her back badly and tried everything he could to win her over. Mom wasn't having any of it. After what happened in Utah, there was no reconciliation of any kind. So, Dad confronted Allen, which led to a fight, and Dad never returned to Virginia. Despite winning the fight, Dad didn't win his woman back. I knew it was really over when I never saw Dad again until three years later. In 1973, Mom and Allen welcomed their daughter, Nikki, into the world.

Dad never really got over his love for Mom, even until the day he passed away. They had an unbreakable bond, despite their ups and downs.

CHAPTER SIX

You're Just the Bastard

The revelation came to light in 1977, a year that holds significance in my memory. It all began the previous year, precisely on August 29, 1976, when my mother sent me and my brother, Rick, on a plane ride from Hopewell, Virginia. Our destination was Florida, a shift that marked a significant chapter in our lives.

Upon our arrival in Florida, our father was the one who welcomed us to Sarasota, where he delivered us to our grandparents' home in Palmetto, Florida. The yearlong interval from our departure from Virginia to this encounter in Florida had a profound impact on me.

Samuel and Vastie Odom were the parents of my father, Joshua Odom. Their humble abode, comprising a modest three bedrooms and one bathroom, accommodated a bustling household of eleven people. Most of their grown children continued to live under the same roof, leaving Rick and me to sleep on a pull-out sofa bed on the screened-in porch, which was a distinctive experience. While the warm Florida climate persisted throughout the year, the nights occasionally brought a cool chill. We snuggled beneath cozy blankets, turning the situation into an enjoyable adventure. It truly felt as though we were slumbering amid nature's embrace, for, in essence, we were, with the absence of a lock on the door.

Those were days when times and the world operated on a different wavelength. We lived in a tightly knit neighborhood, where familiarity among neighbors was the norm. Palmetto was a small city and thrived on its bountiful citrus groves and verdant vegetable farms. It was a rarity for unfamiliar faces to materialize out of thin air, hence our slumber on the porch felt secure. However, the only drawback emerged when it was time for bed. The screened porch functioned as the familial gathering area, where we often spent quality time together. Our bedtime was contingent on the rest of the family retiring for the night, a routine we adhered to even on school nights.

Samuel Odom, who hailed from South Carolina, had to leave the state. He was a Black man who had a dispute with a white man, and because of this altercation, he moved to Florida.

Although he couldn't read or write, Samuel got into construction work, particularly building bridges. He played a role in building the Skyway Bridge in Saint Petersburg, Florida, which unfortunately collapsed on May 9, 1980. This occurred when a six-hundred-six-foot freighter MV Summit Venture crashed into a support column during a sudden squall, leading to the catastrophic failure of over one thousand two hundred feet of the bridge's span. Several vehicles were at the top of the bridge when almost a quarter-mile of roadway fell away beneath them while others drove off the edge because the drivers did not notice the collapse in the driving rain or could not stop quickly enough in the wet conditions. In all, six cars, a truck, and a Greyhound bus plummeted one hundred fifty feet into Tampa Bay, resulting in thirty-five deaths.

After the tragic collapse and the reconstruction of a larger bridge, they repurposed a portion of the old structure into a fishing pier that is dedicated to the memory of the tragic event. It remains a popular spot for fishing because of the vast body of water that connects St. Petersburg to Manatee County.

Samuel Odom, despite his educational limitations, possessed a remarkable ability to handle his finances. He counted his money with precision. Though he could not decipher the written word, he resorted to a simple "X" as his mark when signing his name. The historical use of an "X" as a signature emerged because of limited literacy and language barriers. It indicated agreement or endorsement, particularly among those who couldn't write their names conventionally. He worked long, arduous hours, so most of his interactions were with his wife, Vastie.

Vastie Odom was a straightforward, no-nonsense woman who spared no words and diluted nothing with sweeteners. Born to a slave, Vastie bore the weight of an uneducated upbringing, yet her reservoir of wisdom drew from a deep well of Bible knowledge, street smarts, and innate practicality. She nurtured nine children: Samuel and Mary—who both answered the calling of the ministry, embodying her spiritual legacy—Johnny, Louise, Margaret, Rosalyn, Daniel, Joseph, and Joshua.

Vastie possessed a treasure trove of wisdom. Despite lacking formal education, she brimmed with colloquialisms. Her words, filled with everyday wisdom, reverberated within me, shaping my life's journey.

Vastie was rough on me. Sometimes that roughness was worthy, but most often it was not. She whipped me more than Rick. Often, I stood in and took whippings for him, so he wouldn't have to ensure such torment.

Sometimes she accused me of not washing all the dishes. She says things like, "You should have done this," or "You should have done that," implying that I could have done a better job. The interesting part is that when that person came back into the house, I would be fast asleep. I'd be out on the porch, so they had to pass me to get inside.

Even though they would find a bowl, a spoon, or a glass in the sink, I wouldn't wake up to wash any of it. However, the next morning, when Vastie began cooking breakfast, she'd spot that leftover dish in the sink and start her day by raising her voice about how I hadn't washed the dishes. It became a bit of a routine, her morning complaints about the unwashed dishes.

The intriguing part was that the individual who left the dish in the sink didn't take responsibility for it. They remained silent, not uttering a single word. Instead, they allowed a child to take the blame for leaving the dirty dish in the sink. It makes you wonder if they did it intentionally, considering how their mother, Vastie, was fervent about leaving dirty dishes in the sink.

Our living there added another layer of responsibility for me, as I had to manage my schoolwork and chores. Every Friday, and sometimes on Thursdays, Vastie would wash everyone's clothes, and when I got home from school, both Rick and I had to gather all the clothes, which belonged to three aunts, three uncles, our grandmother, and our grandfather.

That amounted to eight people, including Rick and me, which meant piles upon piles of clothes, including socks, t-shirts, underwear, and everything else. Our duty was to fold and distribute all these clothes, placing them neatly on each person's bed. Along with this, we also had to take care of washing the dishes, making our days filled with various responsibilities.

I often think about the time when Vastie and Samuel generously opened their home to accommodate two additional growing boys. However, because of the lack of space and beds inside the house, we had to sleep on the screened-in porch of their already quite cramped home. Two growing boys meant an increase in the number of mouths to feed.

It's worth mentioning that we didn't receive any form of financial support from our mother, who had sent us to live with Vastie and Samuel. I believe Vastie might have thought we were primarily our father's responsibility, even though he was living elsewhere, with his girlfriend.

Vastie had both a tender side and a contentious nature. The dynamic with Vastie was consistently confrontational. It seemed she had a tendency to belittle me at every opportunity she got, which was disheartening. However, the way she suddenly revealed the information was quite unexpected.

One day, Vastie found herself incensed, maybe because of something I had done. I vividly remember diligently cleaning the modest wooden house, its floors covered with scattered carpets. It wasn't a remarkable dwelling; in fact, it was a rented house. The details of my transgression elude my memory, yet what remains etched within me is the distressing recollection of her unleashing her wrath upon me, an innocent child. Her words, filled with vitriol and malice, pierced through my soul, leaving behind a lingering sense of hurt and bitterness.

"Joshua only has one child," she said to me.

"What are you talking about?" Her words confused me as I struggled to grasp their significance.

"You're not his son. You're just the bastard."

Her words, brimming with animosity, shattered my world within a heartbeat. The revelation hit me like a tidal wave, leaving my spirit crushed beneath its weight. The thought had never crossed my mind that Joshua Odom might not be my biological father. After all, I carried his last name, a symbol of familial connection. But now, I wanted to unravel the truth, to delve deep into the origins of my existence. The need to get to the bottom of it consumed me.

In my confusion, I persisted, asking her to clarify what she meant. She straightforwardly stated that I wasn't born out of a legitimate relationship. Her words left me stunned, and I was only thirteen. I wasn't naïve; I understood the connotation of being called a "bastard." This term wasn't unfamiliar to me, as I understood it referred to my being born out of wedlock.

Samuel Odom—the man who I thought was my biological grandfather, was his stepfather—eventually informed me about the situation, and subsequently, my mother came to Florida for the weekend and engaged in a conversation with me. During this conversation, she disclosed my biological father's first and last name, which essentially summed up the extent of the information she provided. I was so overcome by the shock that I couldn't comprehend or maintain any of the information she had shared in my head. So, as I got older, and was ready to find my biological father, I had forgotten his first and last name.

This was my mother's first and only trip to Palmetto, Florida, to visit her sons. She returned to her life, raising

Nikki, which added to my feelings of abandonment, and I never saw her again until years later, when Rick joined her in Louisiana and begged me to join them.

During this phase of my life, my parents had parted ways, and my dad was living with his girlfriend, Caldonia. As for my mom, she was unavailable, with her whereabouts being uncertain. My recollection of her location is hazy; I believe she was somewhere in the United States because of her government job. During that time, her career had taken off.

Processing this revelation was overwhelming, and I felt compelled to seek the truth from my father. He wasn't living with us but in Sarasota, so I called him. During our conversation, he experienced a moment of emotional vulnerability, leading him to divulge the truth about my birth.

Joshua Odom married my mother, Rachel Ann Walden, in Petersburg, Virginia, on February 28, 1967. This event occurred after I was born on July 31, 1965, rendering me not yet two years of age at the time of their nuptials. Given my tender age, the intricacies of parentage were beyond my comprehension, and I remained blissfully unaware that Joshua Odom was not my biological father. Throughout my upbringing, he was my paternal figure and continues to hold that role in my life, even in death.

During a candid conversation, Dad revealed the truth about my lineage. Dad had lovingly adopted me, bestowing upon me his family name, driven by a profound affection that extended beyond mere blood ties. This revelation illuminated the depth of his love and commitment, reinforcing the unbreakable bond that we shared.

However, this newfound understanding also ignited an enigmatic question: Who, then, is my biological father? An inquiry that remained unanswered, buried beneath layers of time and circumstance. It took fifty-five years, but eventually someone unveiled the identity of the man who contributed to my existence, lifting the shroud of mystery surrounding my origins.

Reflecting on the situation now, the experience must have been emotionally challenging for Dad. Here was a man who willingly assumed the role of a father figure, embracing a young boy as his own, only to receive a distressing phone call that shattered the illusion of a biological connection.

Undoubtedly, this revelation had a profound impact on both of us. He likely wrestled with emotions, recognizing that our bond didn't stem from shared blood but from the authentic care and affection he held for me.

In that situation, his unwavering commitment truly shone through. Despite the unforeseen nature of the circumstances, he stood by my side, offered a listening ear, provided unwavering support, and guided us through the inevitable challenging conversations that unfolded between a father and a son. The way he approached that delicate moment with profound empathy not only revealed the depth of his character, but also underscored the love and understanding that formed the foundation of our relationship. My father, Joshua Odom, died in 1996 from throat cancer.

My mother left my brother Rick and me with Mr. Odom and his family, despite being aware of the circumstances they were living in. She knew things weren't good, but she took no action. We cried out to her, "When are you going to come get us?" She never did.

For years, she promised you would. I remember vividly the year 1976 when we went to visit, the first year she sent us a box for Christmas. It was on August 29. I remember the date clearly. We took an airplane to get there. During that visit, we spoke to her for the first time after learning about the difficult conditions and the challenging situations we were facing. We'd be sleeping on the porch and enduring various hardships. Throughout our time there, we kept asking Mom the same question, hoping for a different answer: "When are you coming to get us?" Each time, she would assure us, "I'm going to come and get you." But as the months went by, and time kept passing, it became clear that these promises were empty. Eventually, we stopped asking because it was clear she had no intention of following through.

I grew up with the feeling that others raised me, unsure of their biological relation to me.

Vastie's Harsh Words of Wisdom

- *You have a long way to go and a short time to get there.*
- *Watch your conduct.*
- *You only get one time to make a first impression.*
- *You reap what you sow.*

- You don't miss your water 'til your well runs dry.
- That little red flannel in your mouth is going to get you in trouble.
- You don't have a pot to piss in or a window to throw it out of.
- You're going to make me bring you down a buttonhole lower
- Tell the truth, shame the devil
- Right is right, and right don't wrong nobody.
- Night ain't got no eyes.
- What's done in the dark will soon come to light.
- God bless you, but Woody's (the local undertaker) going to dress you.
- Don't start something you can't finish.
- Don't start nothing, it won't be nothing.
- It's a poor rat with only one hole.

CHAPTER SEVEN

California Dreamin'

My uncle, Samuel Odom, Jr., Dad's brother, would make the journey from Vallejo, California, to Palmetto, Florida. One summer, Uncle Samuel and his family came for a visit. He and Dad engaged in a conversation during which Uncle Samuel revealed he had recently become involved in the ministry, and quite seriously. He had established a small church in a storefront and was deeply immersed in his new calling.

Uncle Samuel saw that Rick and I were sleeping on the front porch because of the limited space indoors. With my grandparents, Vastie and Samuel, and their offspring, along with Dad's part-time presence, eleven people were living in that house. It was quite a crowded situation. Imagine sharing the bathroom in the morning with all those people. It was quite a challenge, as we had plumbing, but it was always unreliable. We had to keep a five-gallon bucket of water on hand to flush the toilet. The crowded living conditions, with my grandmother's adult children and now Rick and me, added to the pressure on her.

So, during their conversation, Uncle Samuel made a unique request to my father. He asked if he could take Rick and me to California. My father consented, and so we embarked on a journey across the country. With the little belongings we had, Rick and I piled into the back of Uncle Samuel's van as we set out on this adventure. We were excited about going, but we had no clue what to expect or what lay ahead for either of us.

In California, Uncle Samuel had a spacious and attractive home. It was a considerable upgrade from what we were used to. With three boys and two girls now, we initially settled in quite well. Rick and I enrolled in public school in September, adhering to the conditions set before us for this trip.

Prior to our departure for California, there was a specific condition we had to meet. Rick and I sported rather substantial Afros. Our aunt, who was Samuel's sister, used to braid our hair meticulously, which reached down our backs. However, for us to make the journey to California, it was required that we agree to get haircuts. Yes, the price for our trip was a much-needed change in hairstyle.

Our days quickly filled with not just the routines of life, but also a rigorous exploration of the New Testament, encompassing the entire span of the Bible. From the foundational narratives of Genesis to the apocalyptic visions of Revelations, we embarked on a journey of understanding, aided by a quirky song Uncle Samuel and his children composed.

In this newfound household, a clear distinction emerged between us—Rick and me—and them. At the private Catholic school Uncle Samuel's children attended, they enjoyed the privilege of having religious values intertwined with education. They were raised in an environment of exclusivity and discipline, cultivated within these institutions.

Rick and I, however, went to a nearby public school. As the transition from seventh to eighth grade unfolded, our lives became enmeshed in the dynamics of a typical public education system. While the privilege of private education was beyond our reach, I held no resentment; the public-school experience had its own merits and peculiarities that I embraced wholeheartedly.

Our stay in California spanned an entire year, encompassing the entirety of a school term. Our days had a well-organized rhythm and clear objectives: regular family dinners, communal church visits, and earnest participation in Bible study sessions, all of which defined the cadence of our existence.

As the school year neared its conclusion, an incident unfolded that would sow the seeds of change. A pitcher of Kool-Aid, stored in the refrigerator, mysteriously vanished overnight. Without concrete evidence or clues, Rick and I had to account for the disappearance. Suspicion overshadowed our innocence, despite the fact that we had not consumed the Kool-Aid or experienced anything out of the ordinary.

In the wake of this incident, Uncle Samuel made a pivotal decision. Our uncle, the orchestrator of our California journey, told us we had to leave. Our departure was sudden and unceremonious. Packing our belongings and accompanied only by the weight of uncertainty, and one brown paper bag lunch for two, for a five-day trip, we boarded a Greyhound bus—a journey emblematic of the newfound challenges we were about to face. I never understood what happened, but I believe my uncle wanted to help us and give us a better life. Maybe having two additionally mouths to feed was financially too much.

A mixture of anxiety and anticipation coursed through my veins, as we embarked on a five-day journey from the vibrant landscapes of California to the familiar territory of Florida. With no guiding hand, no financial resources, and no provisions, Uncle Samuel cast us on a journey that mirrored the complexities of our young lives.

During our bus ride back to Florida, we forged an unexpected connection. A benevolent older woman on the bus took notice of us.

"Baby, where are you headed?"

Her straightforward yet deep question captured the core of our journey—no clear directions, no money, no provisions, and an unsettling lack of communication with our mother. The whereabouts of our mother remained a mystery to me. Honestly, I wasn't aware if she was aware that Dad had shipped her sons off to the California coast. As we sat on that bus, there was a certain undertone of uncertainty that colored our thoughts.

It's important to note that, during those times, mobile phones were not a ubiquitous tool. Their absence meant that if we were to have gone missing or faced any sort of trouble, there wouldn't have been an instant lifeline to alert others of our predicament. The concept of being disconnected and isolated from the world and those who cared weighed heavily on my young mind.

Yet, during this uncertainty, the benevolent woman on the bus stood as a beacon of empathy and connection. Her simple question, "Baby, where are you headed?" resonated deeply. In those few words, she encapsulated the longing for direction, stability, and the hope that someone, even a stranger, might recognize our existence and extend a compassionate hand.

Her inquiry didn't merely ask about our physical destination, but it probed about the emotional journey we were undergoing. She became the face of empathy in a moment of vulnerability. In her, we discovered a brief yet profound connection, a reminder that amid the unpredictability of life, a genuine human connection has the power to transcend circumstances and offer solace.

Five days later, Rick and I were back to sleeping on the screened-in porch.

CHAPTER EIGHT

Back on the Porch

Upon returning to Palmetto, Florida, I enrolled in Manatee County High School for three years, covering ninth to eleventh grade. Unfortunately, my circumstances remained unchanged.

Eventually, my second departure from my grandmother's house occurred when I was fifteen years old, following an incident involving marijuana and a subsequent physical confrontation. As a result, I had reached a point where I simply could not tolerate staying there any longer.

Dad was involved with his girlfriend, Caldonia, whom I referred to as my mother figure. She fulfilled a more maternal role compared to others. Although she was married, her relationship with her husband was unconventional, and they were amenable to my father's presence. She played a pivotal role in Dad's life, securing an apartment for him, which had two bedrooms. One bedroom Rick and I shared. This became our new living arrangement.

Dad, a Vietnam War veteran, bore the scars of his experiences. This influenced his outlook and behavior. The weight of his history as a veteran and an alcoholic dictated his decision-making.

Dad's family had a tendency to stick together. Despite having multiple adults living in my grandparents' modest three-bedroom house, the desire to strike out independently seemed absent.

Only two individuals left this communal household early in adulthood: Uncle Samuel and his sister, Aunt Mary, who also got married and moved to California.

The reasons behind my father's departure from the house remained puzzling, especially considering he left without taking us with him. He lived there for a few years before our arrival.

We stayed there until conditions deteriorated so much that, at an age where walking away was feasible, I endured a severe beating. Uncle Johnny was in the bathroom, smoking marijuana, and blowing the smoke through the window screen. I was on the outside, inhaling it in. Uncle Joe walked around the corner, saw what was taking place, and told his mother, Vastie.

This infuriated her, and to "teach me a lesson," as I stood between a set of twin beds, Vastie made me take off my clothes, tied together my hands and feet, had me get on the floor, and beat me profusely with a couple of belts, leaving my body welted, bruised, and in immense pain, while my adult aunts and uncles—including the one who blew the smoke in my face—watched on, not uttering one word. Once Vastie had tired herself out, my aunts and uncles said, "You deserved it." I could barely move after such an ass whipping. She whipped me as though I had set the house on fire. I was fourteen years old and beyond humiliated, as my family stood by, watched, and did nothing. This incident marked a turning point in my life. It was time for a change, and I had to be the one to make it.

CHAPTER NINE

Louisiana Bound

Being in Florida, Rick had reached his breaking point and was adamant about reuniting with Mom. She had moved to Louisiana along with my younger sister, Nikki. Rick's desire to be with them was palpable; he longed for a family reunion.

My sentiments couldn't have been more different. Florida was my preferred location, and I wasn't keen on joining Mom in Louisiana. The prospect of being with her didn't resonate with me. Rick went to Louisiana. He spent an entire year there, but his longing didn't wane. Eventually, he turned to me for help.

"Come out here, please," Rick beseeched me.

I was in my senior year of high school and deeply involved in football. The idea of leaving everything behind was difficult to digest. I performed well in school while living with Dad.

However, despite my initial resistance, circumstances pushed me to relent. The pressure Rick applied wore down my resistance, and I eventually agreed to head to Louisiana. Of course, I had my terms. I informed Mom that I'd only consider the move if I could continue playing football. It was a non-negotiable condition for my relocation. She agreed, promising to facilitate my transition in various ways, including enrolling me in school and ensuring I could play football.

So, I made my way to Louisiana, to a place roughly fifty miles from Lake Charles. There, I found myself in a new high school, forging connections with new friends and acquaintances.

However, my presence in Louisiana wasn't solely driven by academic pursuits. Rick was navigating life with Nikki in elementary school. I was in the throes of high school graduation, yet my responsibilities extended beyond the classroom. Mom relied on me to provide a stable presence for Rick and Nikki, acting as a surrogate parent. They needed transportation and supervision, and she entrusted me with these duties. Despite my age, I embraced the role.

Mom recognized my reliability and maturity, which was why she entrusted me with this considerable responsibility. She could travel for work without worrying about the well-being of her children, knowing I could manage things on the home front. While I'd like to credit Mom for instilling my sense of independence, it was my grandmother, Vastie, who played a pivotal role in teaching me self-sufficiency and responsibility, primarily through an abundance of household chores.

Financially, things were tight. Mom would provide me with $40 to cover groceries, but more often than not, our purchases were pre-packaged foods like pizzas. Processed and boxed items dominated our diet, and the only semblance of home-cooked food was the occasional hamburger.

I essentially became the backbone of the household. My time in Palmetto, Florida, living with the Odoms had equipped me with domestic skills. I knew how to run a household efficiently—cleaning, doing laundry, and assuming responsibility. I cultivated this proficiency through necessity. In Florida, we would assist our grandparents with chores, and even pick vegetables and fruit from the fields. Our responsibility was to keep the house orderly. Essentially, we shouldered the domestic load in Florida, and I shouldered it in Louisiana.

This skill set and sense of responsibility that I had gained in Palmetto seamlessly transitioned into my new life in Louisiana.

In Louisiana, I secured a job at Pizza Hut and even had a girlfriend. This newfound life I had constructed felt solid and fulfilling. However, an upcoming change was looming—Mom's job was moving her to Maryland. Yet, I wasn't ready to leave immediately. The idea of leaving behind my girlfriend held a significant emotional weight, and I voiced my reluctance to Mom. Staying rooted in Louisiana felt like the right choice. My connections had grown deep—my girlfriend, my friends from high school, and the camaraderie we shared. Plus, the atmosphere was like Florida's warmth.

As my mother embarked on her journey to Maryland, I made the conscious choice to remain in Louisiana. I lived with a friend, Calvin, and his family. Our bond grew stronger as we spent time together, particularly on the basketball court. The friendship was the full nine yards, deep and meaningful. Calvin had a sister who was significantly older, about six or seven years my senior. Little did I know, she would become the girlfriend I was so intent on not leaving behind.

Calvin's sister held a special place in my heart. What made our connection unique was that she was already a mother of twin girls. Her husband was in the military and stationed overseas. As a result, I gained invaluable insights into the world of women—understanding their needs and learning how to treat them right. Her experience and wisdom were profound, guiding me in ways I hadn't expected. With her six-year seniority, she was a teacher in more ways than one. However, she didn't teach me more than I hadn't already learned.

When I was a young boy, living in Virginia, Mom used to go out with her friends. One friend had a young daughter, who was old enough to babysit me. Each time the girl watched me, she molested me. No one had ever touched me like that before, and at that age, I doubt I understood what was going on. I didn't have anybody to tell. I could tell Rick when he got older, but I couldn't tell Mom because she was not a loving, caring, and affectionate person. She wasn't the mother with whom I felt comfortable sharing my feelings or seeking emotional support. Her maternal approach was distant and aloof and lacked the warmth and openness I had desired. Conversations revolving around personal growth, achievements, and aspirations were rare in our interactions. Unlike the encouraging and motivating parent who instilled a sense of ambition, Mom didn't engage in discussions about excelling or pursuing opportunities. At least, not as far as I was concerned. I see otherwise with Nikki and Rick. However, those aren't my stories to tell.

Her demeanor remained standoffish and remote, creating a barrier between us. The absence of nurturing encouragement or guidance left me without maternal encouragement to explore new avenues or pursue my interests. This void in her parenting approach meant I didn't experience the empowering influence that a mother often provides, urging their child to reach for their potential and embrace new challenges.

I took the initiative and engaged in various activities of my own accord. The sense of independence I developed was self-driven, not a result of her guidance or conversations. Although she attended my athletic events, her presence lacked the motivational aspect of providing encouragement or pep talks. Despite my involvement in baseball, basketball, and football, I never received affirmations like "You can do this" or the typical inspirational talks that parents often give.

As I matured and faced the complexities of growing up, particularly understanding my sexuality, her guidance was notably absent from those aspects of my life as well.

However, I lacked anyone with whom to confide or share my experiences. Neither a father figure nor my uncle Johnnie, whom we called Junie, who was the closest thing I had to a father, could fill that void effectively. Yet, even his presence fell short, as he got entangled in his own complexities. Despite his role as a husband and a father to four children, his behavior didn't set a much better example. His struggles with alcoholism and infidelity played out before my adolescent eyes.

He would occasionally take me along on his motorcycle rides, using these moments to bond. However, these rides led to encounters with various women. We would arrive at their apartments, where he would leave me in the front room while he disappeared into the back with these women.

My upbringing provided lessons through contrasting examples of what to emulate and what to avoid. Despite the clear signs of what not to do, there were still instances of behavior to observe and learn from.

Infidelity marked Uncle Junie's relationship with his wife, Alma, who has since passed away. This pattern persisted throughout their marriage; he was an attractive and charismatic individual, known and respected by many. Despite his amiable nature and charm, he got entangled in extramarital affairs. His night shift work often served as a cover, allowing him to engage with other women. I vividly remember those times when I would return home from school, and he would appear on his motorcycle, whisking me away for yet another episode in his complicated life.

Louisiana became more than just a place I lived—it transformed into a realm of friendships, connections, and unexpected love. The bonds I forged during this period shaped my perspective on life and relationships, carrying lessons that would resonate well into adulthood.

CHAPTER TEN

Gaining My Independence

When my family—Mom, Rick, Nikki, and me—moved to Maryland in 1983, I was eighteen years old. Mom was now working in Fort Meade, and I got a job at Pizza Hut. Rick was still in high school, and Nikki was in middle school. We were all occupied with our own activities.

Having a strong desire not to be at home, I had little trust in Mom. We didn't have a relationship where we talked about our aspirations or plans for the future. I can't recall her ever encouraging me or asking what I wanted to do with my life. From a young age, I knew I wanted to become a police officer, a dream that had been with me since I was about nine or ten years old.

Coming to Maryland presented an opportunity to pursue my dream. However, I didn't join the police department. Instead, I enlisted in the military, specifically the U.S. Navy. Oddly, I didn't even discuss my decision with Mom. She wasn't involved in the process at all.

Life in the military was enjoyable, and I relished the chance to travel. I went to California for boot camp. The Navy provided structure and discipline, although it took some getting used to in the beginning. During that initial period, we learned the ropes and could not take leave or liberty. It was all about learning the rules and regulations.

I formed long-lasting friendships during my time in the Navy. For example, one of my closest friends, Allen, who hailed from North Carolina, remained a good friend even after we left the service. Allen trusted me to drive his car while he was intoxicated, a decision that led to a car accident. I thought Allen's father would be furious, but surprisingly, Allen and I remained friends.

The Sum of Me

In the Navy, I met various people from diverse backgrounds, traveled the world, and had unforgettable experiences. The military shaped me into the person I am today.

CHAPTER ELEVEN

Enter Roy Waiters

This chapter remains succinct as my knowledge about Joshua Odom's biological father, Roy Waiters, is limited. While he may not be my biological grandfather, he still represents a small yet significant fraction of the mosaic that forms the sum of who I am. So, Joshua Odom was not raised by his biological father, but was raised by Samuel Odom as his own. Rachel Walden was not raised by her biological father, but was raised by Johnnie Walden as his own. And together, as my parents, they decided to raise me the same way, with the secrecy of not telling me Joseph Brundage was my biological father.

Regrettably, details about Roy Waiters are scant, leaving a void in my understanding of this familial lineage. Despite the gaps in knowledge, the acknowledgment of his existence becomes a critical puzzle piece in unraveling the intricate narrative of my roots.

Roy Waiters' presence, though subtle in the bigger picture, adds to the overall influences shaping my identity. By acknowledging his role, even if not well-defined, I realize the interconnectedness of family ties that go beyond the immediate and familiar. Although the details of his life story are unclear, recognizing his impact, though indirect, emphasizes the intricate network of influences that contribute to who I am. This brief acknowledgment serves as a reminder of the diverse nature of familial connections, even when some aspects remain unknown.

After Mom sent Rick and I to Florida to live with Dad's, Joshua Odom's, parents, Vastie and Samuel Odom, we learned Samuel was not our actual grandfather, nor was he Dad's biological father. It turned out that Roy Waiters was our true grandfather. I believe Joshua was around forty years old when he made this discovery.

Someone asked if Dad knew about Roy Waiters. I'm not entirely sure how he found out, whether he encountered Roy at a local bar or on the street, but somehow it all fell into place. Dad introduced us to Roy while they were both quite intoxicated. I was around fourteen years old, making Rick about twelve. That was how we came to learn about our true family.

This revelation also meant that we had more relatives, including cousins we didn't know about, and a broader extended family. Two of these cousins even played in the NFL. I discovered this later in life, as Vastie, Samuel, or Dad didn't speak about this topic.

There seemed to be a common theme on both sides of my family: the biological fathers were unknown. Family members concealed certain truths when it suited their purposes or circumstances and selectively decided when it was fitting or necessary to reveal these secrets to a child. It appears they did so without a single consideration of the potential harm or emotional impact it could have on the child for the entirety of his life.

CHAPTER TWELVE

Feeling Unloved

Allow me to begin this chapter by emphasizing that my primary goal in writing this book was never to criticize, hurt anyone's feelings, or disgrace anyone. My aim was simply to share my experiences and perspectives, hoping to help someone else. However, it's important to acknowledge that one person's truth might not always paint others in the most favorable light.

I remember my childhood vividly, even though it often feels like I was a world away from the child I once was. Growing up, I never felt loved by my mother, but I understand she didn't know how to show something she had never experienced herself. The love her mother might have given her vanished when she passed away during my mom's early years.

The absence of maternal love defined Mom's life, leaving an unfillable void. It was like attempting to paint a masterpiece without ever having seen a color, a seemingly impossible task. And that void extended to my upbringing, casting a long shadow on our relationship. Coupled with the knowledge that Johnnie Walden was not her biological father, and to my knowledge, she knew nothing about her biological father, it's funny she chose to keep me in the dark.

From my earliest memories, Mom had difficulty expressing her love. I longed for her affection, but it felt like trying to grasp a distant star. I yearned for warm embraces, soothing words, and that comforting feeling of knowing that she cherished me, but they were always just out of reach.

As a child, I couldn't comprehend the complexities of my mother's emotions. It wasn't until later in life that I understood her struggles. She had lost her own mother at a tender age, leaving her emotionally scarred. Without the guidance of a maternal figure, she was ill-equipped to provide the affection and emotional support that a child so desperately needs.

Instead, she expressed her love in different ways. Mom often busied herself with household chores, an attempt to show she cared through her actions rather than her words. She made sure to meet my needs, keep my clothes clean, and keep our home in order. I see now that she was expressing her love in the only way she knew how.

In our strained relationship, my mother's love was like an unspoken language, a code I struggled to decipher. It wasn't until adulthood that I came to recognize her sacrifices and her efforts to provide for me and my siblings. Her love was not conventional, but it was real in its own unique way.

Despite the void that existed between us, I now understand the depth of Mom's love. She may not have been able to express it in the traditional sense, but she made countless sacrifices to give me the best life she could. She didn't talk much about her love, but she integrated it into every aspect of my upbringing.

As an adult, I've chosen to embrace the love she provided, to appreciate her for the sacrifices she made, and to show her the affection she never quite knew how to convey. In doing so, I've learned that love, no matter how unconventional or unspoken, can bridge the gap between hearts and heal even the deepest of wounds.

CHAPTER THIRTEEN

Tracing Roots and Family Secrets

I joined Ancestry.com because I had a big question on my mind: Who was my biological father? I wanted to know if I had any brothers, sisters, cousins, or other family members out there. The problem was that my mother never told me anything about him, and I couldn't gain access to my original birth certificate, which usually has this kind of information.

So, I turned to Ancestry.com as my best shot at getting answers. It seemed like a great place to dig into my family's history and maybe find some clues about my biological father.

With the help of Ancestry, I hoped to piece together the story of my family and hopefully find the missing parts of my past.

Subscribing to the top-tier membership on Ancestry.com grants you access to a trove of records: marriage certificates, birth certificates, military service records, and various other public documents. This is how we got the marriage certificate.

When I started building my tree on Ancestry, I received my first connection. Her name is Rhonda, and she lives in Ohio. She says, "I think we're related."

Once we connected on Ancestry, we shared our contact details. Since both of us had provided our phone numbers and email addresses on the platform, Rhonda left her phone number there for me. When I was heading home from work, I called her.

Then, she launched into "I have information." She had been on Ancestry.

I immediately became intrigued and asked, "What information?"

She asks about my mom's name, to which I replied, "Rachel."

She followed up with, "And her maiden name?"

"Walden."

That's when she dropped the bombshell—she found evidence of my mom's marriage to Joseph Brundage.

Clearly, I felt shocked. All my life, I'd only known about one marriage, and that was to Joshua Odom. Surely, she had to have been mistaken. I said, "Wait, what?"

She detailed how the pieces fell into place. Then, Rhonda said she was close with Joseph's sister, Tiny, and they stayed in touch regularly. This connection led to my sister, Toni Brundage, entering the picture, as Rhonda shared Toni's phone number with me.

I reached out to Toni, and our communication began in October 2021. We started exchanging messages and information, laying the foundation.

It's worth noting that I'm not aware of Toni being on Ancestry or any social media platforms. Instead, she had a connection with Aunt Tiny, who played a crucial role in connecting Toni to me. She made a call and said, "I think we've found your brother, Toni." That's how everything fell into place.

Joseph Brundage was married to Toni's mother. This new revelation to Toni put Mom and Joe's marriage in Winchester, Virginia, before I was born.

Interestingly, when Mom was seven months pregnant, she traveled to Virginia to marry Joseph, only to give birth to me a mere two months later in Pittsburgh, Pennsylvania. This brings up a perplexing question: Why did they go to Virginia for the marriage when they were both living in Pittsburgh?

The complexity deepens when, after giving birth, Mom didn't leave her father's house until she took me, piled us up in Uncle Junie's car, and moved to Virginia. Her entire life seemed to have revolved around Pittsburgh, though.

Strangely, Mom never openly acknowledged this marriage. The glaring question here is: Why didn't she declare her marital status and live with her husband?

One plausible reason could be that her stepmother and father were keenly aware of Joseph's wife, where they lived (just around the corner), and various other essential details.

From San Diego, Toni played a pivotal role in organizing the reunion, even though she couldn't attend.

On December 4, 2021, she started the process, even though it was still during the school session. We were all eager to meet, and Toni took charge of the arrangements.

She contacted each of her aunts—Ollie, Berniece, Tiny, Sis, and a close friend—organized the meeting location in Pittsburgh, and even made restaurant reservations all the way from San Diego. They also had a close friend they considered like a sister who wanted to join, too.

When the day came to meet my long-lost family, I was excited and curious about connecting with people who shared my family tree. As the moment neared, I felt a bit nervous and anxious, unsure about how I would be received and if things would match my expectations.

Ariane and I spent some time in the car outside the restaurant, observing everyone entering and wondering if they were relatives. At one point, a woman entered with a man young enough to be her son, and we both said, "I bet she's an aunt and he's a cousin." Turned out, we were right. It was an aunt with her son Justin, who she adopted. We were so taken by his attentiveness to her every need. Yet, another example of how bonds don't have to be biological.

When we finally met, a wave of joy and relief swept over me, and I felt a deep sense of belonging. Finding shared traits, stories, or even physical resemblances brought us closer and made me feel whole. I couldn't help but feel grateful for the chance to fill in missing pieces of my personal history and to build new connections with people who were once strangers but now mean a lot to me.

When we all gathered at the table, we called Toni, as she had requested, and she wanted us to take lots of pictures to document the moment. Yes, Ariane took many pictures. I was living in the moment, smiling, and overwhelmed with a sense of closure, a sense of finally knowing not only who I am but *whose* I am. We have quite a collection of them.

Growing up, I attributed much of my traits and attributes to Mom, whom I resemble in many ways. It is a common jest among us to say that I could easily resemble her if I just wear a wig and shave my mustache.

However, what truly left us jaw-dropped was when Ariane and I we delved into family photos the aunts brought, revealing where my distinctive qualities truly originated. Surprisingly, many of these characteristics did not trace back to Mom, but to Joseph Brundage, my biological father.

Learning about these newfound similarities between me and Joseph Brundage was a remarkable experience. From his love for water, swimming, athleticism, and even his choice of cologne and fashion—the connections ran deep.

That day was special; I felt a sense of completeness. It marked a turning point in my story. Everyone shared their knowledge and stories, and I got to see their initial reactions to meeting me. They pointed out my unique voice, mentioning how much it resembled that of their brother, Joseph Brundage. It was a remarkable moment of recognition, something I had longed to hear for years—no, my entire life.

They even inquired if anyone had recordings of his sermons, as he was a minister. However, no one could remember having any recordings of his sermons. The gathering deeply moved everyone, and I believe it was a profound experience.

While there, Ariane received a phone call from her mother, and she stepped outside the restaurant to take it. She was trying not to disrupt the moment, to keep this connection intact.

However, upon returning inside, she shared the news that an ambulance had taken her father to the hospital. It was then that Ariane and I witnessed something truly extraordinary. Our newfound family stopped everything, dropped what they were doing, held hands, and prayed. They embraced us, offering their support and prayers, even though they barely knew us. What's even more astonishing is that the entire restaurant came to a complete stop and joined us in prayer. It was a deeply spiritual and emotionally charged moment. Their heartfelt response showed the strength of their faith and the warmth of their hearts. They prayed for us without knowing the full extent of our family's history, and it was incredibly moving.

Joseph Brundage, our father, was a man of faith who took his role as a father very seriously, despite the challenges he faced in connecting with his children. Learning of his efforts to find and reunite with me left an indelible mark on my life. It was not a simple case of abandonment; he was determined to maintain a connection with me, even though he faced obstacles like sealed birth records.

Toni spoke of how he was the best father in her eyes, highlighting his dedication and commitment to his family, even in the face of an uncertain future. His wife, her mother, was aware of my existence and was willing to accept me into their family, but once my mother packed me up and moved back to Virginia, he couldn't find me.

The last image Aunt Sis described of ever seeing me was a poignant one. "I walked into my mother's house," she recounted, "and there was this precious baby in a beautiful blue blanket on her lap. Intrigued, I asked, 'Whose baby is that?' and my mother replied, 'This is Joe's baby.'"

The introduction to me had been a heartwarming moment, but it turned out to be the last time she saw me. Unfortunately, Aunt Sis died on June 6, 2022. It was an honor and a blessing to have had the opportunity to meet her before she passed.

Ariane couldn't bring herself to tell me about her father's situation until after we left the restaurant. Sadly, my father-in-law had passed. I had lost a father-figure on the same day I had a special connection to my biological father and family. We shared over twenty years of love admiration and lots of laughs. Ariane still says that Dad helped the Pittsburgh Steelers win the game. The following year, he had spoken about how they weren't doing so well, but we won the next year. We also had plans to attend the Pittsburgh Steelers football game against the Baltimore Ravens the following day.

Since we hadn't been to the new stadium in Pittsburgh before, a friend of Ariane's sold us tickets for the game. When she and her husband heard about the passing of Ariane's father, we ended up spending most of the following day, Sunday, at their house.

We had an incredible time with them, and their hospitality was heartwarming. Her husband, whom I had bonded with over our shared experiences as veterans, sadly passed away a year later. Despite not being surrounded by the familiar faces we would usually draw strength from in times of grief, that experience is something Ariane and I often reflect upon because our familiar faces usually look to us for strength, but in this instance, we were in a different role.

Unfortunately, the football team we were supporting was not performing well that year, but we won against the Baltimore Ravens. We were just one game away from making it to the playoffs, but our team's inconsistency held us back throughout the season.

By May 2022, after many calls, it was time to visit Toni face to face. Right before we were ready to go to California, I received a leaf hint that seemed to connect me with a young blonde Caucasian girl who Ancestry identified as my second cousin.

This revelation was puzzling. I tried to piece together how this girl, who lived in San Diego, California, could be my second cousin. I questioned Toni about whether her father's brother had ever lived in California, and it turned out that he had spent about a month there during his high school years before heading off to college. This prompted us to wonder if he had left behind any family ties during his visit.

I called the girl to learn more. She explained that her mother was white, and her father was biracial, but her father had been adopted, and they had no information about his biological family. This conversation led to a breakthrough when I suggested her father take a DNA test to uncover a genuine connection.

Ancestry's DNA matching algorithm assumes second cousin status based on the percentage of shared DNA. This means that only one-eighth of their shared DNA is being recognized as relatedness, and categorizing the rest as second cousin level. However, the girl's father took the DNA test, and, low and behold, her father, Aaron, is my half-brother, making her my niece.

This revelation left me stunned, as it, once again, uncovered long-held family secrets. I was also concerned about Toni's reaction to this revelation. We shared a great week together, bonding, sightseeing, and getting to know each other. The most remarkable sight was to see the base where I did my naval basic training on, and to know that my father worked in a building so close to where I had laid my head was unnerving. How did we never meet in 1985? What would have happened if we had met? Maybe I wasn't ready. Maybe he wasn't ready.

While we were in San Diego, we organized a meeting with all of us, but before that, we shared photographs. When Toni saw the pictures, she instantly recognized the family.

Toni had once observed a family in a restaurant while she was eating alone. She thought their close-knit and diverse family was amazing. They remind her of a family she knew in Japan, who jokingly called themselves the "Polka Dot Family" because of their varied hair and skin colors, which was their way of embracing their differences. This encounter had left a lasting impression on Toni, even though she hadn't interacted with them.

Surprisingly, both families lived not far apart on the outskirts of San Diego, California. So, of course, we invited Aaron to the family dinner. When my niece asked if her grandfather could join our dinner, we gladly agreed, not realizing he would play a pivotal role in uncovering the truth.

A Puerto Rican mother and an African-American father, who couldn't have biological children, adopted Aaron as an infant. The adoption agency they used had extensive records, including social notes and interviews. Aaron's adoptive father brought these documents with him to dinner, revealing that they had always offered Aaron the opportunity to search for his biological family.

However, Aaron had initially declined, not wanting to face potential rejection or unknown family dynamics. Out of love and respect for his adoptive parents, it was only after his adoptive mother's passing that he explored the possibility of reconnecting with his biological roots.

Surprisingly, Aaron located his biological mother first, but unfortunately, he faced rejection. She was a white woman who worked at a church and was married to a white man. She had kept the fact that she had given him up for adoption a secret.

Aaron also connected with a first cousin and an aunt through Ancestry. These relatives were more receptive and actively helped him establish a connection. They provided him with a direct phone number, but the biological mother clarified that she didn't want any further contact. This rejection deeply affected Aaron, and he discontinued his exploration.

Then, unexpectedly, Aaron's daughter used Ancestry and connected with me. Toni, who is deeply religious, found herself in a state of disbelief. Both Aaron and Toni are devout believers, and Toni attempted to piece together the puzzle. She learned Aaron's age, and his location in San Diego, and then a crucial piece of information emerged.

Aaron's adoptive father, while reluctant to delve into this matter, had brought important documents with him. These documents contained psychosocial information and interviews that revealed the story of how Aaron came into existence. Joseph and his mother had met and worked together on a military base, engaging in an affair over some time. Also, her family, who were Canadian, had moved to San Diego but held strong racist beliefs. Her name was Terri, and when Toni read that name, it triggered a memory.

Toni recalled a traumatic incident from her high school years involving her mother and Terri, which marked the end of her parents' marriage. An argument had erupted in their home, and Toni had mistakenly believed it was about a man named Jerry from her father's job at the base. For years, she had thought Jerry was the cause, not realizing it was actually Terri. This revelation led to her parents' divorce.

In contrast to my situation, where the family was aware of my adoption by Joshua Odom, they never brought up Aaron's existence with his two siblings. They had grown up as a family unit, unaware of Aaron's existence. Toni and others in the family read the documents, which Joseph had written, explaining he had two children heading to college and couldn't financially support a newborn baby.

It was clear from the documents Joseph didn't want to give up Aaron, but believed it was the only viable option because of financial constraints. This added complexity to Aaron's quest, as he was the secret child with whom Joseph had lost touch. In contrast, Terri, Aaron's biological mother, had no other children, making Aaron her firstborn.

She had to make the painful decision to give him up for adoption primarily because of her father's influence. This family history and the circumstances of Aaron's birth highlighted the societal norms and challenges faced during that era, particularly in the 1960s and 1970s, when Aaron was born. It marked a significant contrast between Aaron's and my experiences growing up.

After Joseph and his first wife divorced, he moved on to his second marriage, in which he wed another woman who also lived in San Diego. Unfortunately, they faced fertility challenges and adopted an infant. It's ironic how Joseph played a role in both losing a son through adoption and gaining a child through adoption—Robert.

I've never had the chance to meet Robert because he passed away. Then, Toni was living in San Diego alone, having lost her mother, her brother Joe, whom I wasn't able to meet before his passing, and her half-brother Robert. Joe and Robert had grown up together, living close to Joseph's first wife and

Toni. They were practically family, with Toni even babysitting Robert. Toni's mother had been a source of support whenever needed, forming a strong bond between the two ex-wives and the three children. This deep connection among them speaks to the importance of love and commitment to each other until the end.

Toni continues to maintain contact with the children, considering them her nieces and nephews. She sends them small gifts and tokens of affection, keeping the family connection alive. This stands in stark contrast to Joseph's third wife, Catherine, who did not share the same bond. Catherine, despite becoming a minister like Joseph, lacked warmth and affection.

So, during Joseph's second marriage, he attended seminary school and became a pastor. By the time he returned to Pittsburgh, he was an experienced minister with a church in San Diego. When he introduced Toni to Catherine, his third wife, they had two daughters and a son. Toni received an unwelcoming reception during her last visit. Her mother and father remained good friends, which Catherine strongly disliked. As for Joseph's second wife, I'm unsure if he maintained a friendship with her, but the first and second wives remained close.

Toni initially had trouble processing all of this information. She isn't active on social media and isn't heavily involved in Ancestry-related activities. So, it took some time for everything to sink in. However, as memories resurfaced and pieces fell into place, she finally saw the connection. She looked at Aaron's hands and confidently said, "You are my brother." Ariane tells Aaron he hit the jackpot with amazing siblings, and he says, "I couldn't agree more!" So, I have a relationship with Aaron now, and he and Toni share a strong bond. He has been very supportive, assisting us with various tasks and offering his help whenever needed. Toni is no longer alone in San Diego; she has a brother who is there for her, as well as his wife and children.

I would like to believe I played a pivotal role in bridging this family gap by connecting Toni with Aaron.

CHAPTER FOURTEEN

Navigating Secrets and Quest for the Truth

The remarkable parallels between me and my biological father, Joseph Brundage, are nothing short of astonishing. Our shared characteristics, common interests, and even a striking resemblance in our younger years create an uncanny connection that extends beyond the physical into aspects of personality, mannerisms, life choices, and even our voices. Even without knowing or meeting him, Joseph Brundage's essence feels deeply intertwined with the core of who I am.

Unbeknownst to me, my life journey mirrored that of Joseph Brundage's, as I followed in his footsteps by joining the Navy. At a certain point, we were both stationed in San Diego, even at the same base. Despite our proximity, our paths never crossed. It's a curious thought—had they intersected, would I have recognized him? Would I have realized I was essentially looking in a mirror? The likelihood is minimal, if not nonexistent.

This profound connection with Joseph Brundage becomes even more poignant considering his absence throughout my life. His passing occurred before I could fathom his existence, leaving me with a void that time has struggled to heal. The enigma of our shared traits, forged through the strands of genetics, leaves me grappling with the mystery of how such profound similarities could manifest without direct influence.

With the assistance of my newfound sister, Toni Brundage, I've delved into the intricacies of our shared characteristics, finding echoes of his persona in my quirks, habits, and worldview. The uncanny alignment of interests, shared sense of humor, and parallel approach to life's challenges all bear the indelible mark of Joseph Brundage, despite our worlds never colliding in a tangible sense.

The passing of Joseph Brundage severed the prospect of a conventional father-son relationship, yet the echoes of his existence persist in my own.

In my earlier years, I believed Joshua Odom to be my biological father, only to discover the truth in a revelation from the woman I considered my grandmother. This disclosure, made in a moment of anger, sparked an intense yearning to unravel the mystery of my true paternity. The question of "Who is my father, and where can I find him?" echoed incessantly in my mind.

Mom deliberately kept my biological father's identity a secret, creating a significant gap filled with unanswered questions about my background. The silence around his presence, combined with the awareness that he wished for a connection with me, adds complexity to the emotional fabric of my life. Before my maternal grandparents passed away, they disclosed Joseph Brundage's desire to keep and raise me with his family. This choice was strongly opposed by my mother, prompting our move from Pittsburgh to Virginia.

As I think about this intricate narrative, my goal is not to assign blame but to shed light on the complex emotions inherent in the human experience, particularly when influenced by family secrets and revelations. The ongoing effort for forgiveness, understanding, and acceptance mirrors the continuous pursuit of truth and the strength required to recover from the impact of withheld information. The dedication to openness is apparent in my resolve, as a father, to ensure my sons are aware of their heritage and the guiding figure in their lives—a commitment rooted in the profound hurt caused by the lack of such transparency in my own upbringing.

CHAPTER FIFTEEN

Walking in Faith

Religion plays a profound and integral role within the African American family, serving as a resilient source of strength, identity, and community. Rooted in a history marked by struggle, resilience, and triumph, the religious experience has been a cornerstone, offering solace, empowerment, and a sense of belonging.

The African American religious journey in the United States has diverse roots, with influences from traditional African spiritual practices, Christianity introduced during the era of slavery, and subsequent developments within various Christian denominations.

Churches have been more than places of worship; they have been sanctuaries of communal support, education, and activism. The Black church, in particular, has played a pivotal role in shaping the African American religious experience. It has been a haven where the community could gather not only for spiritual nourishment but also to strategize and mobilize for civil rights and social justice.

The religious practices within African American families often extend beyond Sunday services. Family members participate in church auxiliaries, community outreach programs, and religious education classes. The teachings of faith permeate everyday life, influencing moral values, work ethics, and familial bonds. Prayer becomes a collective practice, providing a foundation for resilience in the face of adversity.

The music born from the African American religious experience, such as gospel and spirituals, has transcended the walls of the church, becoming a cultural expression that resonates far beyond religious contexts. These musical forms, with their powerful lyrics and emotive melodies, serve as a testament to the enduring faith and unwavering hope within the African American community.

Religion has also been a force for individual empowerment. Many African American leaders, from Harriet Tubman to Martin Luther King Jr., drew strength and inspiration from their faith as they led movements for freedom, equality, and justice. The intersection of religion and activism continues to be a driving force in addressing contemporary issues and fostering community upliftment.

Despite the diversity of religious affiliations within the African American community, a shared sense of spirituality often transcends denominational boundaries. Whether within Baptist, Methodist, Pentecostal, or other Christian traditions, the overarching theme is one of seeking a connection with the divine that imparts strength, resilience, and a sense of purpose.

In essence, religion is not just a facet of the African American family; it is a dynamic force that has shaped, sustained, and propelled generations forward.

Like many families, religion plays a significant role in mine, forming a lasting connection that spans across generations. Faith has played a substantial role in shaping our lives, values, and beliefs, with its foundations deeply rooted in the unwavering devotion of my maternal and paternal grandparents.

My maternal grandparents, Johnnie and Dorothy Walden, stood as pillars of faith in our family narrative. Their home, during my upbringing, was a sanctuary of prayer, love, and a deep commitment to their religious beliefs. Active members of Macedonia Church, they attended services faithfully and took part in various church activities.

Dorothy, my maternal grandmother, was renowned for her steadfast dedication to her religious convictions. As elaborated earlier, she not only taught Sunday school but also sang in a gospel trio. Her focus on God was palpable in her actions, with her heart and eyes wholly devoted to her faith.

Equally committed, Johnnie, my grandfather, served on the Male Usher Board and in the Male Chorus, earning respect as a revered figure within the congregation. Their bond, strong both as a couple and as spiritual partners, exemplified a shared journey of faith.

My mother, Rachel, embarked on her unique faith journey, finding a home in the Seventh Day Adventist Church—a distinctive Christian denomination known for its emphasis on Sabbath observance on Saturdays and a commitment to a health-focused lifestyle. Mom's daily display of a mustard seed pin on her lapel became a silent yet powerful reminder that even the smallest seed of faith could move mountains. Her involvement in organizations like the Eastern Star, with its unique expression of Christianity, shaped her belief in the diverse ways she could live by faith.

The spiritual influence extended to my paternal grandmother, Vastie Odom, whose extensive knowledge of the Bible, wise quotes, and street-smart wisdom left a lasting impact on me, even if not fully appreciated during my early adolescence.

As life unfolded, I embarked on my quest for spiritual understanding. Drawing from the lessons of my mother and the unwavering faith I witnessed in my grandparents, I explored various forms of faith and religion in search of a personal connection with God.

An unexpected revelation emerged when I discovered that my biological father, Joseph Brundage, was a minister, adding a profound layer to my spiritual exploration. This newfound connection offered a unique perspective on faith, enriching my understanding in unexpected ways.

Whether symbolized by a mustard seed pin or the words of a father who was a minister, faith remains the thread that binds us—a legacy that continues to shape our lives and values. I could not have made it where I am without my faith in God. With Him, I am no one.

CHAPTER SIXTEEN

My Two Sons

A pivotal moment in my life occurred when I became the father of two incredible sons, Mark Junior and Branden. This life-changing event prompted a profound transformation within me. I became acutely aware of the kind of father I aspired to be, particularly because I had my share of challenges stemming from fatherhood. I was resolute in my commitment to always be there for my children, regardless of the circumstances. The unwavering consistency of Ariane's and my cell phone numbers for a quarter-century stands as a testament to our unwavering stability and commitment. This unwavering stability ensured that our children never had to wonder about my whereabouts or endure prolonged periods of uncertainty.

I wholeheartedly embraced the role of a father, and I fought diligently to secure visitation and custody to ensure our sons could be together, despite having different mothers. My foremost goal was to foster a deep bond between them, and I constantly encouraged them to look out for each other. The importance of expressing love was a value passed down to me by my grandmother, Vastie. While my father, Joshua Odom, seldom voiced his love, he showed it through his actions.

I made it a point to instill in my sons the significance of saying, "I love you" to each other before concluding their conversations. Regardless of any other life changes or decisions, I remained unwavering in my dedication to my role as a father. I consistently prioritized my children and made time for them, even amid the demands of my work hours. Ariane and I adjusted our schedules to ensure we could spend quality time with them, and we enthusiastically shared our hobbies and interests with them.

Our children readily adopted many of my hobbies and interests, including a shared enthusiasm for dirt bikes, cars, swimming, and sports.

Having experienced the painful disconnection from my own biological father, I was determined to break this longstanding family pattern. The thread of separation ran through generations, starting with my great-grandmother to my grandmother to my mother, all of whom didn't know their biological fathers. I was resolute in my desire to shield my sons from this disheartening cycle. I yearned to be an integral part of their lives, with a firm belief that no child should endure the emotional turmoil of not knowing their biological father.

I understood the additional anguish that surfaces when a mother withholds a child from their father. I was unwavering in my commitment to be an involved father, and I refused to allow my sons' mothers to place me in a position where I couldn't connect with my children. My determination stemmed from the desire to create a different and healthier family dynamic for my sons, ensuring that they would never have to endure the pain of a fractured father-child relationship.

Ariane played an invaluable role in shaping my sons' upbringing. She exhibited unwavering love and care, never treating them as anything less than her own children. Her dedication and warmth have left an indelible mark on their lives. I genuinely believe that I owe much of my personal growth and the father I have become to her unwavering presence by my side. Words alone cannot express the depth of gratitude and affection I hold for her. She is nothing short of remarkable in every aspect, and I couldn't love her more.

Now, we have the incredible joy of being grandparents, a role we cherish immensely. This new chapter in our lives has filled us with excitement and anticipation. Being grandparents has opened up a world of possibilities and the opportunity to create lasting memories with our grandchildren. We delight in taking them on camping trips, fishing adventures, and various escapades that bring us closer together. These moments of bonding, exploration, and shared experiences are not only immensely gratifying but also add a new layer of fulfillment to our lives.

As parents, we believe we have set a positive example for our sons when it comes to parenting. Witnessing them embrace fatherhood with love and responsibility is a source of immense pride. Their dedication to their own children reaffirms the values and principles we've instilled in them, and it warms our hearts to see them grow into exceptional men.

CHAPTER SEVENTEEN

My Ride or Die...and Then Some

"I had a list of criteria for a partner, and Mark ticked every box. I didn't want someone who had already been married. Mark had been previously married. I didn't want a partner with children, as he already had kids. And I definitely didn't want to marry a police officer. He was intent on being the po po. But in the end, it turned out that he was the best thing that ever happened to me."

–Ariane Odom

In 1998, I tied the knot with my best friend, Ariane, marking the beginning of our evolving relationship. As is the norm in any long-term partnership, both of us underwent changes over the years. Our story takes a fascinating twist when we recount the events of our Valentine's Day date with a friend that eventually led to us confessing our feelings for each other and even starting an LLC. This became a pivotal moment in our commitment to one another. We decided to take the plunge and get married later that year on November 25, which was not our initial plan.

Our house situation heavily influenced the change in our wedding date. We had discovered a house we were eager to purchase, secured buyers for our previous home, and originally set our wedding date for February 14. However, circumstances unfolded rather unexpectedly, and we advanced our wedding date to November 25. This change in plans came about during a casual visit to Wendy's on November 24, where, on a whim, I suggested we should get married. And just like that, we made up our minds and headed to the courthouse, the next day we were officially married. Our wedding day was an unconventional one, featuring a Wendy's meal complete with chili and a chocolate Frosty.

For my proposal, I used yellow napkins from Wendy's, and as a special memory, we continued to use yellow Wendy's napkins during our anniversary dinners for many years. The particular Wendy's location was situated near our soon-to-be home, which we had previously visited before making the purchase. We spent twelve years living in that house. Following our Wendy's visit, we proceeded to the courthouse, where we completed the marriage license application process. It's worth noting that you don't get married on the very same day you obtain a marriage license, so visiting the courthouse in Annapolis was a part of the overall procedure.

Obtaining our marriage license held particular significance because of Ariane's part-time job in retail, a field that offers no respite after Thanksgiving, especially during the chaos of Black Friday. Fortunately, she had secured the week leading up to Thanksgiving off, and her boss readily agreed, understanding that she would work tirelessly afterward.

However, our house situation added an unexpected twist to our plans. The seller canceled the settlement, which led us to consider tying the knot during our week off. We still planned to have the official ceremony in February.

In the end, we got our marriage license, and the very next day, we made our way to the courthouse for a simple and meaningful wedding ceremony. As soon as we stepped out of the courthouse, Ariane's phone rang. It was our realtor, thrilled to announce, "Settlement is on. Settlement is on." We hurried to the office, not only to take care of business but also to pick up the girls who were purchasing the house. They were renting a house across the street from us. They lived in Baltimore, lacked a vehicle, and needed transportation to settlement.

We reached out to the girls with the exciting news that we had just gotten married and arranged to pick them up at six o'clock. At the office, the seller of the house had become indecisive about the whole situation. While she initially liked us, our kids, and our love story, she was now having second thoughts. She was planning to move to Florida, but her move was postponed until January. She proposed renting her house back from us, but this arrangement didn't align with our plans. With two kids and a dog, and considering the need for our home's new owners to move in, we couldn't accommodate her request.

Eventually, we worked out an agreement where I allowed the girls to live in my rental property, and we rented the house back to the seller. However, things took an interesting turn when the seller realized the significantly higher rent she would be paying. This led her to neglect the commitments she had made regarding the house's maintenance. Adding to the complexity of the situation, during the settlement, we were required to sit in separate rooms, with individuals shuttling back and forth to exchange documents. The seller refused to share the same table with us during the house sale.

This whirlwind of events led to us getting married on the very same day we sold one house and bought another. It was a situation that no one would intentionally plan. To this day, I'm unaware of anyone else who has experienced a situation quite like ours.

Besides dealing with the canceled settlement, we also had to address our transportation situation. My engine blew up in my car days before settlement while going to have lunch with Ariane. This led to us purchasing a Toyota 4Runner the next day. In summary, our journey began with a flurry of challenges that demanded our attention and problem-solving skills. We navigated the complexities of having children from different mothers, along with a dog. However, we overcame these challenges and made our relationship work. Twenty-five years later, we are still together, a testament to our enduring love and commitment.

Throughout our journey, Ariane and I have faced our fair share of challenges and triumphs, which have contributed to the enduring strength of our relationship. Like peanut butter and jelly, we complement each other in a way that goes both ways, and I wholeheartedly believe in the reciprocity of our bond.

Our shared interests in fishing, the great outdoors, and travel have been integral in maintaining the robust connection we share. These common passions have not only deepened our bond but also provided us with cherished memories throughout the years.

Furthermore, our educational backgrounds played a significant role in forging the strong foundation of our relationship. Ariane graduated with a degree in sociology, with a concentration in corrections, from Towson University, while I graduated with a degree in criminal justice from Coppin University. This shared background created a profound connection between us, fostering an understanding and synergy that has been a cornerstone of our enduring love.

Our relationship has always burned with an intense flame, one that has remained unwavering as the years have passed. Through the ups and downs, we've continued to thrive, our shared experiences and interests fortifying the deep connection we share. We coined the phrase, "From mole to soul." She is my soulmate.

CHAPTER EIGHTEEN

Mom and the Next Generations

Some of the following is to show the generational disparities that I have felt, not just for myself but also for my children. As we delve into the story, I've provided all the intriguing details and anecdotes about various family dynamics. However, the underlying point is to highlight certain qualities we've already discussed, such as a lack of nurturing and consistency. It's essential to recognize that while my mother may not have been nurturing to me, she has displayed nurturing qualities toward Nikki's children, much like she did with Nikki. Nikki never left her side. She didn't send her off to be cared for by Allen's family. Nikki always knew her father's identity.

From the beginning, the separation in treatment was apparent, going back to when I was thirteen years old. This separation has persisted throughout my life, affecting not only me but now extending to the next generation. However, there is a significant difference when it comes to the younger generation. Mom has wholeheartedly embraced and supported the two oldest of Rick's five children.

Notably, Mom embraced Rick's oldest two children because she had a longstanding bond with their mother, who was also Nikki's close friend. This deep connection allowed her to treat those children as if they were her own. She took them with her on her travels, and they became well-traveled individuals.

Rick's children from his second marriage or former relationship did not receive the same level of care. In those cases, the mothers did not facilitate a relationship between the children and Mom, and as a result, did not form a deep connection.

When Ariane and I got married, our family dynamics were different because of the presence of my youngest son, Branden, who was only two years old, and my mother would not spend time with my son because of his age. My mother shared her perspective on family, gatherings, and other aspects of our lives, emphasizing how it was a unique experience for her compared to her interactions with the older generations of children in our family.

Her comment to Ariane was, "Oh, I don't do that," meaning she did not take them on outings and did not let them spend the nights at her house, like the other grandchildren. This was when she lived in Baltimore and Ariane and I lived in Glen Burnie. She explained that she didn't take care of children that young. She preferred to wait until they were old enough to look after themselves.

I believe there's a deep-seated resentment towards me because of my biological father and him not choosing her. Joseph Brundage stayed with his first wife and two children. I think my mother always knew he was married, considering that both the Brundages and Waldens were practically neighbors. Plus, she was friends with the sisters. It's hard to believe that she wouldn't know he was married. I think that deep resentment might be at the root of the issues.

Although I'm not an expert in psychology, sociology, or any related field, I believe that's what's happening here. This is what I aim to convey to readers. There are certain characteristics that become apparent as you read through the generations, and I have observed and understood these because I'm now an adult and a parent.

Here's a story that illustrates the situation: both she and Nikki bought a timeshare in Orlando together, but they kept it a secret. We had no idea about it until their plans were almost in motion, and they needed my assistance. They called and asked, "Hey, Mark, can you drive a fifteen-passenger van down to Orlando for us?" I was essentially being asked to provide Uber-like services. Yet again, it wasn't the initial occasion on which I was requested to dedicate my time to their advantage. After all, they are my mother and sister. Why wouldn't I lend them a hand? My only desire is for that assistance to be reciprocated.

Mind you, neither Ariane nor my two sons were going on this trip. They wanted me to drive them and their selected grandchildren to Walt Disney World. When I questioned this request, they didn't even see the problem with it. They justified it by saying, "Oh, your kids have been there." This is the same justification they've used for many things.

They simply assumed they could rely on me, that I'd be fine no matter what. Fast forward to the next generation, and they had the same mindset: "We don't need to worry about your kids; we know you'll make sure everything is taken care of." The same line of thinking extended to the next generation through her interactions of lack of interactions with my grandchildren.

Mom frequently compared her treatment of different grandchildren and made habitual statements that became unbearable. In the end, I couldn't take it anymore. Among the first two grandchildren she favored, Courtney, who is the oldest. Courtney has a daughter who is the same age as my granddaughter, and they attend the same school. Although Mom was closer to Courtney, she distanced herself from her as well.

When she was closer to her, she was aware of every stage and every comment. For instance, if I mentioned that my granddaughter learned to ride her bike this week, she would respond by saying my great niece had been riding her bike for two weeks. This would happen every time we talked.

When Mark, Jr., and Kelsey were expecting, Mom couldn't attend the baby shower. Instead, she came up two weeks after the baby shower and took them shopping, allowing them to pick out whatever they needed that they didn't receive at the shower, and then meeting them at the register.

CONCLUSION: HIDDEN TRUTH

In our family, keeping things under wraps was common. It was the norm. In my parents' and grandparents' generations, they believed in keeping certain things unspoken, without considering how those secrets might impact others. My mother chose not to share details about my biological father. As these secrets came to light, it brought forth a mix of challenges affecting how I feel, think, and inability to trust others.

Finding out that my biological father's identity was intentionally kept from me hits hard. It was not just stumbling onto some hidden truth; it's like realizing there's a crack in the trust I thought I had with my mother. I mention this because it wasn't someone else's duty to inform a child about his father when that child belongs to another woman. That responsibility should fall on the mother's shoulders—my mother's shoulders.

At first, it's confusion—why would they keep this from me? The feeling of being unintentionally betrayed is tough to shake. The revelation messes with my head, messing up the idea that we're open with each other in this parent-child thing.

This confusion turns into frustration, and it's even more intense because I find out my own mom chose to keep this secret. I want to understand my own story better, hoping to fill the gap left by this missing information. Questions about who I am, where I come from, and how I fit into everything hang there without answers.

Underneath it all is an unspoken kind of hurt—a loss for the family story that we could have had. The chances to know, to have connected with my biological father, slipped away, leaving me with this emotional gap that's hard to put into words.

As these feelings unfold, it's not just learning something new; it's like being on a rollercoaster of confusion, frustration, and silent hurt. The trust in our family came undone, which set the stage for me to figure out who I am and how to deal with all this emotional stuff.

To conclude, here's what I believe: my mother loves me. I don't know all of her traumas, failed relationships, bad choices or the repercussions because of her choices that make her who she is or why she treated me the way she did.

Yet, I've chosen to navigate this emotional weight by becoming a different parent to my sons and grandchildren. In my journey, outlined in *The Sum of Me*, I've deliberately worked to break the cycle, ensuring that the love and support I provide reflect the nurturing I yearned for but didn't fully receive. Everyone's identify and family matters. Don't withhold the information.

Starting my quest for independence, I enlisted in the U.S. Navy, a choice that revealed a familial connection with my biological father, Joseph Brundage, who also served in the Navy. My mother could have told me my biological father was also in the Navy, but she failed to do so. Later in life, I would learn that Joseph Brundage also served in the U.S. Navy.

As an entrepreneur, I engaged in diverse ventures, including real estate transactions, cell phone sales, and bail bondsman.

Reaching a pivotal milestone, I earned a Bachelor of Science in Criminal Justice from Coppin State University, setting the stage for a fulfilling career in law enforcement that will lead to my retirement.

Marriage to my best friend, Ariane, and raising my two sons, Branden and Mark, Jr., enriched my personal life beyond professional accomplishments.

My commitment to service extends beyond the obligations of my professional roles, encompassing volunteering, mentoring, and the establishment of a scholarship program—an homage to the enduring impact of education. Despite relational challenges, my grandmother imparted invaluable life lessons. The scholarship foundation, named in honor of Vastie Odom, holds profound significance as a representation of my acknowledgment of the lessons learned from her, even in the face of adversity.

My grandmother's narrative, as a child of slaves denied the opportunity for education, highlights historical injustices.

Despite adversity, she emphasized the enduring value of education. Naming the foundation after her serves to perpetuate her legacy, drawing attention to the transformative power of education and recognizing the resilience displayed by individuals like my grandmother, who were denied this fundamental right.

Strong in faith, I remain actively involved in my community and church. I strive to lead a purposeful and balanced life, embracing a commitment to both personal and societal well-being.

Family

Joseph Brundage, my biological father.

My sister, Toni Brundage

Maternal grandfather, Johnnie "Buddy" Walden, Sr.

Maternal grandmother, Dorothy Walden

A young Mark Brundage Odom.

Biological father, Joseph Brundage, school photo.

My son, Mark Jr., the fourth generation

Three generations of Brundages

Mark and brother, Rick.

Mark Brundage Odom, vacationing in Dubai.

Mark, Sr., Ariane, Mark, Jr., and Branden

Mark and Ariane

About the Author

Hailing from Pittsburgh, Pennsylvania, and having traversed the globe in his formative years, Mark Brundage Odom now proudly resides in Maryland with his beautiful wife, Ariane.

In *The Sum of Me*, Odom embarked on a profound journey to piece together the intricacies of his identity and trace his roots.

www.ingramcontent.com/pod-product-compliance
Lightning Source LLC
LaVergne TN
LVHW041844070526
838199LV00045BA/1425